"And God made the beast of the earth according to its kind, cattle according to its kind, and everything that creeps on the earth according to its kind. And God saw that it was good."   GENISIS 1:25

AuthorHouse™
1663 Liberty Drive
Bloomington, IN 47403
www.authorhouse.com
Phone: 1-800-839-8640

© 2014 Janet K. Warren. All rights reserved.

No part of this book may be reproduced, stored in a retrieval system,
or transmitted by any means without the written permission of the author.

Published by AuthorHouse 3/14/2014

ISBN: 978-1-4918-7324-3 (sc)
978-1-5049-0074-4 (hc)
978-1-4918-7323-6 (e)

Library of Congress Control Number: 2014904793

Print information available on the last page.

Scripture quotations marked NKJV are taken from the New King James Version. Copyright
© 1982 by Thomas Nelson, Inc. Used by permission. All rights reserved.

This book is printed on acid-free paper.

Because of the dynamic nature of the Internet, any web addresses or links contained in this book may have changed
since publication and may no longer be valid. The views expressed in this work are solely those of the author and do
not necessarily reflect the views of the publisher, and the publisher hereby disclaims any responsibility for them.

authorHOUSE®

Dedicated to my good friend and fellow bibliophile, Vivian Lilley, who not only shares my love of reading, but reads what I write.

"But now ask the beasts and they will teach you; And the birds of the air, and they will tell you." Job 12:7

Mahlah the Mouse and Baby Jesus

"And she brought forth her first born Son and wrapped him in swaddling cloths, and laid Him in the manger, because there was no room for them in the Inn" LUKE 2:7

A very long time ago, in fact it was well over 2000 years ago; there lived a little brown mouse whose name was Mahlah.

Mahlah lived under a manger in a small stable behind an Inn, in the little town of Bethlehem. The stable was a lovely peaceful place and all the animals that lived there were Mahlah's friends.

The stable was quite small, but it was home to a horse, a donkey, three sheep and two goats, as well as a black cat named Jesher and of course, Mahlah the mouse. Even Jesher was Mahlah's friend and although he usually liked to catch mice, Mahlah was his good friend.

Gera and Kesia, the innkeepers were very kind. Every day, they would bring food for all of the animals in the stable and even made sure that there were a few scraps of food left under the manger for Mahlah.

One day, two people and their donkey came to stay in the stable. The animals that lived in the stable were a bit nervous because they were not used to having people in the stable, except for Gera and Kesia.

The donkey that came with the two people was named Demas. Demas told the animals in the stable that the people were Mary and Joseph. He said that they were very kind and good to all animals, including mice, so the animals shouldn't worry. Demas also told them that Mary was about to have a baby! That was especially exciting for Mahlah because she was expecting to have some babies.

The very first night that Mary and Joseph were there, baby Jesus was born! It was the most amazing thing. A star appeared right after the birth that night, so bright, it lit up the sky right over the little stable. Then angels came to visit, telling the animals that this child was the Son of God Himself. The angels then went to tell everyone about baby Jesus.

The animals could tell that baby Jesus was very special. Mahlah scurried up the leg of the manger and looked down at the wonderful child. Mary smiled at Mahlah, knowing that soon Mahlah would be a mother too. All of the animals were so excited about the new baby and they cooed and hummed to soothe baby Jesus to sleep every night.

Each day, people came to see this wonderful Son of God, but the nights were usually quiet, so that baby Jesus could sleep. The animals slept too, after baby Jesus was settled for the night and even Mary and Joseph slept in the peaceful stable. Jesher the cat, who preferred to sleep during the day, kept watch over everyone while they slept.

One night, while everyone slept, Mahlah gave birth to six tiny mouse babies. They were all healthy except for the tiniest of them and Mahlah was very worried. She asked Jesher to watch over the other five babies and she carried the tiny one she named Phebe up into the manger.

Phebe was not even moving, but Mahlah was hoping that Jesus, the Son of God, would be able to help her little one.

When she climbed onto the manger, Jesus stirred from his sleep and looked at Mahlah and Phebe and smiled. Jesus could not speak yet of course, but He knew that Phebe needed help.

Jesus put out His tiny hand and nodded to Mahlah to put tiny Phebe into His hand. Mahlah did this and prayed for Phebe. Jesus closed His tiny hand gently around the baby mouse and closed his eyes. Something very special happened. Baby Phebe began to move!

When baby Jesus opened His eyes and His hand and smiled again, tiny Phebe lifted her head to Mahlah and smiled! Mahlah felt so blessed to have six healthy babies she and prayed her thanks to God. Mahlah knew that Phebe would be fine now and carried her back under the manger to where Jesher had been watching over the other baby mice.

Phebe curled up with her brothers and sisters and slept peacefully, with her mother Mahlah curled up around all of them and Jesher watching over them.

When Mary saw the babies the next morning, she smiled at Mahlah even though she did not know about the wonderful miracle that had happened that night after the baby mice were born.

Laban the Lamb and Shemuel

"So it was when the angels had gone away from them into heaven, that the shepherds said to one another, "Let us now go to Bethlehem and see this thing that has come to pass, which the Lord has made known to us."" LUKE 2:15

A very long time ago, in fact it was well over 2000 years ago; there lived a little white lamb named Laban.

Laban was the youngest lamb in the herd of sheep that were looked after by Shemuel the shepherd. Shemuel loved all of the nearly one hundred sheep he looked after, but he had a special place in his heart for Laban.

Laban was the smallest of all of the sheep, so Shemuel worried about him. He was afraid that Laban would get hurt or not be able to keep up with the other sheep, when he took them up into the hills to eat the fresh grass.

Laban himself was a little worried too, but he did his best and tried very hard to keep up with the older and bigger sheep. When Laban couldn't keep up, Shemuel would pick him up and carry him.

There was a special hill the herd of sheep liked to graze on. It was lovely and warm in the sunshine on the good days, and when it rained, there were trees that would keep them dry.

Most days were pretty much the same for the herd. During the day, the sheep would eat the grass and drink what water they could find. At night, they would lie down and sleep.

There were also several other shepherds in the area with their own herds that would come by and chat with Shemuel and Laban.

Not much changed from day to day, until one night. It was a very clear night and the sky was filled with millions of tiny little stars. Suddenly, there was one very bright star that appeared over the nearby town of Bethlehem! This was very strange and the star was so bright that all the sheep woke up and Laban even jumped into Shemuel's arms.

Shemuel and Laban and all the shepherds and sheep just stood there looking at the bright star, wondering what it meant. Was something going to happen? Had something already happened?

While they looked up to heaven at the bright beautiful star, suddenly an even brighter light appeared very close to them! This light was so very bright, that the shepherds had to cover their eyes. Laban was so scared; he hid his face against Shemuel and started to shake.

This light was not another star, this was an angel! The angel said to them, "Do not be afraid. I bring you great news. This is wonderful news to all people. Tonight, in the town of Bethlehem, a Savior, the Son of God, has been born. You will find him in a tiny stable, wrapped in soft clothes and lying in a manger."

Then the whole sky was filled with angels! They were all singing, "Glory to God in the highest. Peace and goodwill to all!"

Then as quickly as the angels appeared, they all disappeared back to heaven and the sky was, as it had been, with millions of beautiful little stars and one very bright one over Bethlehem.

Shemuel and the other shepherds were very excited! They decided to leave all of the sheep on the hill and go to Bethlehem to see the Son of God. Shemuel knew he must take Laban with him, so he hurried along with the other shepherds into Bethlehem, carrying Laban.

As the angels had told them, they found the Son of God asleep in a manger in a little stable in Bethlehem, with his mother and father, Mary and Joseph. Shemuel told Mary and Joseph what the angels had said.

Mary told the shepherds that the baby's name was Jesus. All of the shepherds then bowed down to the baby and thanked God for sending His Son.

Shemuel gave little Laban to Mary as a gift to the baby Jesus. Laban was very proud and felt very special to stay with this very special baby in the little stable.

As Shemuel said goodbye to Laban, he said that all of the shepherds would go back to their flocks of sheep and pray their thanks to God for all of the things they had seen and heard that night. What a special night and what a great gift all the people had, in this wonderful Son of God, who was Savior to all the people.

Tirza the Horse and the Three Wise Men

"And when they had come into the house, they saw the young Child with Mary His mother and fell down and worshipped Him. And when they had opened their treasures, they presented gifts to Him: gold, frankincense and myrrh." MATTHEW 2:11

A very long time ago, in fact it was well over 2000 years ago; there lived a beautiful, black horse named Tirza.

Tirza was a tall, proud horse owned by Serug. Serug and Tirza would often be hired to guide people and caravans through the desert and from city to city.

Tirza thought that this trip was the most exciting of all. Tirza and Serug had been hired to guide three wise men and their caravan to a place under a beautiful bright star. It was a strange request, but Tirza could see the star in the sky and knew that it had to lead to a very special place.

Tirza was a little nervous about this trip when they first started out though. There were so many animals and people in this group, including other horses and donkeys too, but the wise men were riding three huge camels, which were much bigger than Tirza and she was not used to camels.

This journey was going to take several days and the very first night, Tirza found herself at the water trough with the three camels. The camels introduced themselves to Tirza. Their names were Gamul, Hashum and Telem and although they were much bigger than Tirza, they were very kind to her.

The three camels told Tirza of the many adventures they had been on with the wise men. They said that the wise men were Caspar of Tarsus, Melchior of Persia and Balthazar of the city of Saba. This journey was to find a new baby king that would be found under the bright new star in the sky and the three wise men were bringing gifts to the new king.

It was a very long and dusty trip through the cities and towns, but Tirza lead the group proudly at night, so they could clearly see the star they needed to follow.

One day, the three wise men stopped to visit King Herod, since they were passing through his great land. When the wise men returned from their visit with King Herod, they continued on their journey. As they continued on, they talked about King Herod.

Serug and Tirza listened while they talked about telling King Herod of the great new king they expected to find when they got to the place under the great star. They thought that King Herod might join them and also bring a gift, but Herod just asked that they report back to him about this new king.

Tirza continued to lead them towards the star and one night they arrived at the little stable in Bethlehem where the baby Jesus was born. The wise men said they had been expecting a great palace or perhaps at least a fancy house, but the baby Jesus had been born in a simple stable.

Tirza watched as each king bowed before the baby and laid a gift by His manger. Caspar gave the baby Jesus a casket of gold; Melchior gave myrrh, a very special sap from a rare tree and Balthazar gave the baby frankincense, also a very rare sap with a wonderful smell.

Serug also bowed before the baby Jesus and Tirza could tell how special this baby was. Tirza could see how proud all the animals in the stable were including a mouse and her little babies and a black cat. All of the stable animals were very excited that they had been part of this very special event.

The visit of the wise men was now over and everyone got ready to go home. The three wise men got ready to return to King Herod to tell him of the great king they had found.

As they left Bethlehem, a beautiful angel appeared in the sky right above Tirza. Tirza was very frightened but the angel told her not to worry. The angel just needed to tell them not to return to King Herod because he was very mean and he only meant to hurt the baby Jesus.

Tirza promised the angel that she would return the three wise men home by a different road that would take them around the great lands of the mean King Herod.

Serug told Tirza that he knew that this would make King Herod very angry; he said he knew that King Herod did not like it when he was disobeyed.

Gideon the Goat and Joseph

"Joseph also went up from Galilee, out of the city of Nazareth, into Judea, to the city of David, which is called Bethlehem, because he was of the house and lineage of David." LUKE 2:4

A very long time ago, in fact it was well over 2000 years ago; there lived a little brown and white goat named Gideon.

Gideon was a determined little goat who was born and raised in a little stable in Bethlehem. Gideon lived in the little stable with a horse, a donkey, three sheep and another goat, Eglah his mother, a little mouse named Mahlah and a black cat whose name was Jesher.

Every day in the little stable was pretty much the same. Gera and Kesia, the owners of the Inn, would come into the stable every day and feed all of the animals. During the day, the animals all played together while Jesher napped, and at night, the animals all slept, while Jesher watched over everyone.

Gideon loved all the animals in the stable. They were all good friends with each other. Except for Gera and Kesia, the animals didn't see people very often.

One day that all changed.

Bethlehem seemed busier than usual and Gideon knew that Gera and Kesia were really busy because they only rushed in to feed the animals and were saying to each other that the Inn was filled with people for the first time in a very long time.

Then late one day, Gera and Kesia brought two people and their donkey, Demas, to stay in the little stable. Gideon listened while Demas explained that the two people were Mary and Joseph and that he had brought them on a long journey to Bethlehem. Demas also told them that Mary was expecting a baby any day, so he had carried her carefully on his back the whole way from Nazareth.

Everyone settled down for the night, but then things got even busier! Mary gave birth to baby Jesus that night and all the animals knew that He was a very special baby. Even Gideon could tell that He was special. A beautiful bright star appeared high in the sky above the stable, right after the birth.

Demas explained to Gideon that Mary and Joseph had talked about the special baby as they journeyed from Nazareth. The newborn baby was actually the Son of God! Gideon was then determined to always protect the baby Jesus, so he always slept between the manger where baby Jesus slept, and the door to the stable.

Over the next weeks, Joseph noticed how determined Gideon was to keep the baby safe. Joseph was very happy of that because the little stable became a very busy place. Joseph liked to pay special attention to little Gideon because Gideon was doing such a good job of watching over baby Jesus.

The very night of the birth of Jesus, the shepherds from the hills outside Bethlehem came to see this miracle. One of the shepherds brought a little lamb named Laban, as a gift to the baby. One night three wise men came and brought gold, frankincense and myrrh. Many others came to see the Son of God, but Gideon made sure that it was always quiet at night, for the baby to sleep.

Now Gideon was just a little goat, but very determined to make sure that the baby Jesus was safe. Because of that, Joseph made sure to let Gideon know just how proud he was of him.

Not long after the three wise men came to visit, there was a bright light in the stable that woke everyone! It was an angel with a message from God to Joseph. Gideon listened as the angel told Joseph that he must take Mary and the baby Jesus and run away to hide in Egypt! Gideon knew he had to help.

Gideon listened as the angel explained that King Herod had become very angry that the three wise men had not reported back to him after seeing the Son of God, so he was going to send soldiers to look for the baby Jesus. Joseph needed to hide baby Jesus until he was told it was safe to return to Nazareth.

Mary and Joseph gathered all of their belongings and prepared to leave the very next day. Gideon followed Mary and Joseph out of the stable with Laban.

Joseph was happy that Gideon wanted to go with them because he knew that Gideon would always make sure that baby Jesus was safe. Laban would also be a good help and both Gideon and Laban had become good friends with Demas, their donkey. Even though it was a journey away from their home of Nazareth, Joseph knew that everything would be fine. God's creatures would make sure of that.

Naarah the Goose and Elizabeth

"But the angel said to him,"Do not be afraid, Zacharias, for your wife Elizabeth will bear you a son, and you shall call his name John.""   LUKE 1:13

A very long time ago, in fact it was well over 2000 years ago; there lived a lovely little white goose by the name of Naarah.

Naarah lived with a very old woman named Elizabeth and her very old husband Zacharias. Elizabeth and Zacharias had both prayed for children, but had never been blessed with them.

Zacharias was a priest at the temple and because he was at the temple in Jerusalem most of the time, Elizabeth had made friends with Naarah, the little white goose. Naarah was good company for Elizabeth, since she had no children and Zacharias was busy at the temple every day.

One day, when Zacharias left for the temple, Naarah followed him. This was very strange, but since Zacharias knew he would be alone in the temple that day to burn the incense, he was happy to have the company. Naarah waddled along quietly behind Zacharias into the temple.

After Zacharias had lit the incense, a bright light appeared and frightened both Zacharias and Naarah. Naarah waddled up close to Zacharias looking up at the bright light. The bright light was an angel, who had a message for Zacharias!

Naarah listened carefully, while the angel told them not to be afraid, "I am Gabriel." said the angel. "God has listened to your prayers, Zacharias. I have come to tell you that Elizabeth will have a son. You will name him John."

Gabriel then said, "John will be very special and will tell many people about God. This will help to get everyone ready for the arrival of Jesus, the Son of God!"

Naarah believed what Gabriel said, but she could tell that although Zacharias believed in and prayed to God, he could not believe the angel Gabriel. Zacharias said that it was hard to believe this was true because he and Elizabeth had waited so many years for children and they had given up waiting.

Gabriel said,"I was sent by God to tell you this news, but since you do not believe me, you will not be able to speak until the baby is born." Then the angel disappeared as quickly as he had come.

As Zacharias and Naarah left the temple, he tried to tell everyone the great news, but the angel was right, he could not say anything!

Naarah could not believe that the angel had been so mean. How could Zacharias tell Elizabeth the wonderful news if he could not talk? Naarah knew that she must stay very close to Elizabeth until the baby came. Naarah was very excited about the baby that would soon be part of their family.

When Elizabeth discovered that she was going to have a baby, she and Zacharias were very excited and Naarah was so very happy to be part of the excitement.

While Elizabeth was waiting for her baby John to be born, her cousin Mary came to visit to tell her that she would also have a baby. Naarah knew that both Elizabeth and Mary were going to have very special babies, blessed and sent by God. It was a very exciting time!

The day that baby John was born, all of their family and friends gathered to celebrate the birth of this miracle. Elizabeth and Zacharias had waited for so many years to be blessed with a child, and he was finally here. Naarah was so excited that she waddled excitedly around everyone who came to visit! Naarah flapped her wings and honked! She had never been so excited!

Since this baby was the first born son to Elizabeth and Zacharias, everyone expected his name to be Zacharias, after his father, but Elizabeth said, "No, his name must be John!"

Everyone said that there was no-one in the family by the name of John and turned to Zacharias to ask him what the baby's name was to be.

Zacharias still could not speak, so Naarah pushed over a writing tablet with her beak. On the tablet, Zacharias wrote, "His name is John!"

That is when the next miracle happened! Zacharias could now speak! Naarah now knew that Zacharias not only believed the miracle of the birth of the child he and Elizabeth had waited so many years for, but that this baby was specially sent by God and named John and would bring the word of God to all who would listen.

Naarah was so very excited about how very blessed their little family was.

Abda the Monkey and Simeon

"And it had been revealed to him by the Holy Spirit that he would not see death before he had seen the Lord's Christ." LUKE 2:26

A very long time ago, in fact it was well over 2000 years ago; there lived a very cheeky little monkey by the name of Abda.

Abda was the cheeky friend of a very dear old man named Simeon. Abda and Simeon lived in Jerusalem and spent much of their time at the temple there. God had told Simeon that although he was over 200 years old, he would not die until he had seen the Messiah, the Son of God.

Now Abda went to the temple every day with Simeon, hoping that Simeon would finally meet the Son of God that God had promised him he would see.

Abda, being a very cheeky monkey, would run around the temple quite misbehaving as monkeys will do. But Simeon enjoyed watching silly Abda and Abda was at least careful not to touch anything he shouldn't. Watching Abda helped Simeon to keep busy, while he waited every day at the temple. Simeon knew that one day; the Son of God would come into that very temple.

Even though Abda was very cheeky, he loved Simeon very much and when Simeon would kneel down to pray, Abda would do his best to be a good little monkey and sit very still perching on Simeon's shoulder. Sometimes it was awfully hard for Abda to be still, but he tried his very best, because he loved Simeon and liked to make him happy.

As Simeon prayed, Abda would fold his little monkey paws together, just like Simeon would fold his own hands. Then Abda would bow his head and listen to Simeon's prayers.

Abda heard Simeon thank God for all of his many blessings and pray that soon the Son of God would come so that he could see him and know that the special child had been born.

One day, while Abda was behaving his very best and Simeon was kneeling to pray in the temple, a man and a woman walked into the temple with a baby. Simeon stood up from kneeling so quickly that Abda nearly fell off his shoulder!

Simeon walked quickly toward the baby, with Abda on his shoulder.

Both Simeon and Abda knew that this baby was very special. Abda tried not to get too excited, but he was really pretty sure that this baby must be the Son of God. This must be the baby that Simeon had been waiting so patiently for!

The man and woman introduced themselves as Joseph and Mary and told Abda and Simeon that the baby was Jesus and had been named that by an angel that visited Mary before the baby was born.

Simeon took the baby Jesus from Mary and said to Him, "I have waited all my life for You to come! I praise and thank God for letting me see You, that I may die in peace. Praise be to God!"

Simeon then turned to Mary and Joseph and said "Bless you! This child was chosen by God to be the Savior of the world. But I warn you that it will not be an easy job for Jesus. Many will be mean to him and it will make you very sad."

Abda looked down on the baby Jesus from Simeon's shoulder and smiled at the special child. Abda could tell how very happy Simeon was to have finally seen the Son of God.

Just then an old woman by the name of Anna came over to speak to Mary and Joseph. Like Simeon, Anna was at the temple every day, so Abda knew her. She was a prophetess. That meant that she delivered messages from God.

For many months, Abda heard Anna telling all who would listen, that the Son of God had been born and would soon come to the temple. Abda had heard her tell everyone many times, but he had not seen the Son of God until now.

Now, Abda knew that the Son of God was a very special child that would have a very difficult job, but would be the Savior of the world. Abda was very proud to have met the baby Jesus, but he was especially happy that Simeon had finally been able to meet the Son of God.

All creatures, great and small, thank you for sharing their stories and pray that every day everyone will include God's creatures in their own stories.

CPSIA information can be obtained
at www.ICGtesting.com
Printed in the USA
LVOW01s1351081115

461575LV00006B/24/P

9 781491 873243